Olga Goloveshkina

The queens. Monsters. Werewolves. Goddesses.

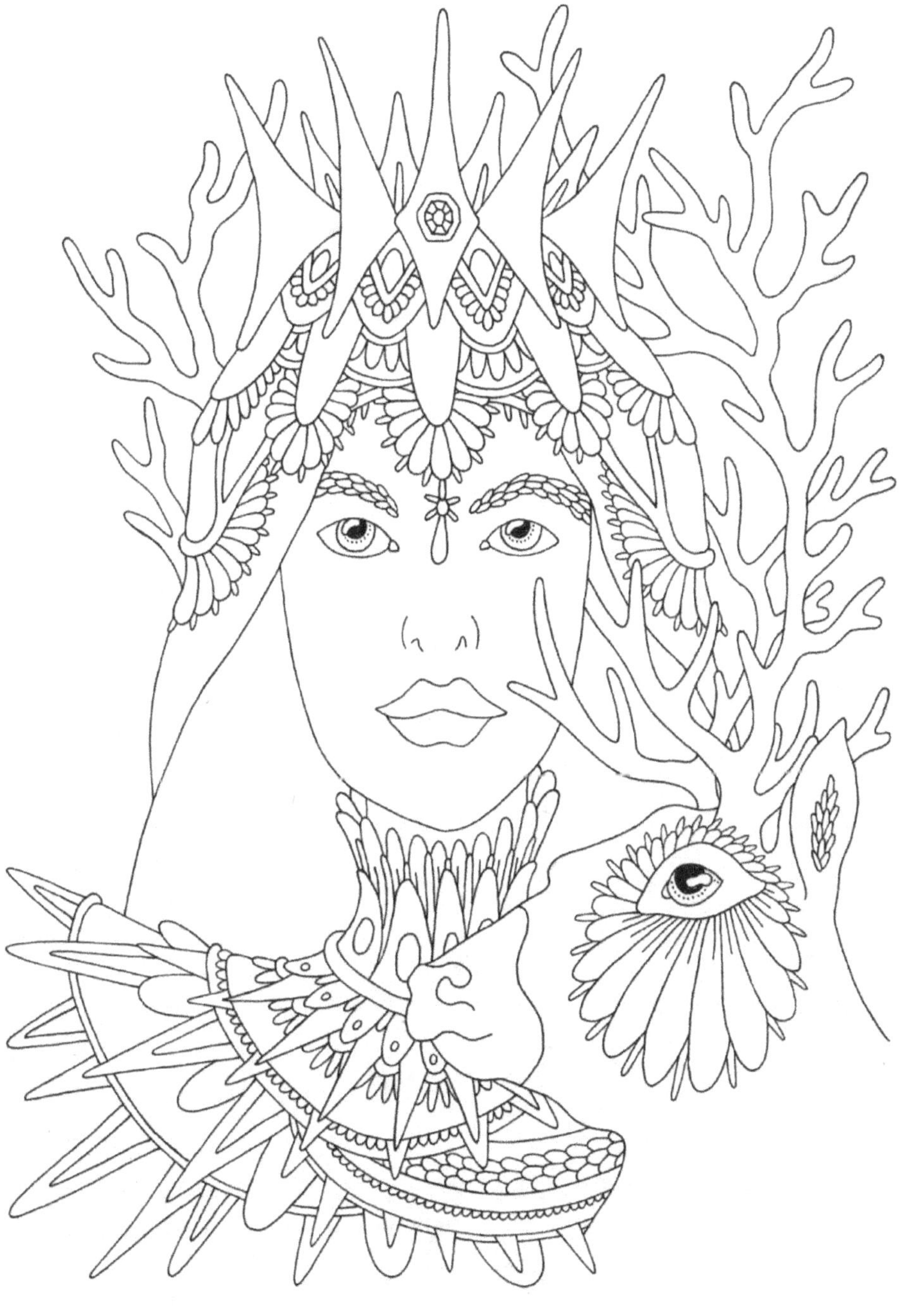

Stress Relief Coloring Book: Adult Coloring

Copyright © 2018 Olga Goloveshkina

All rights reserved.

ISBN: 1987719212
ISBN-13: 9781987719215

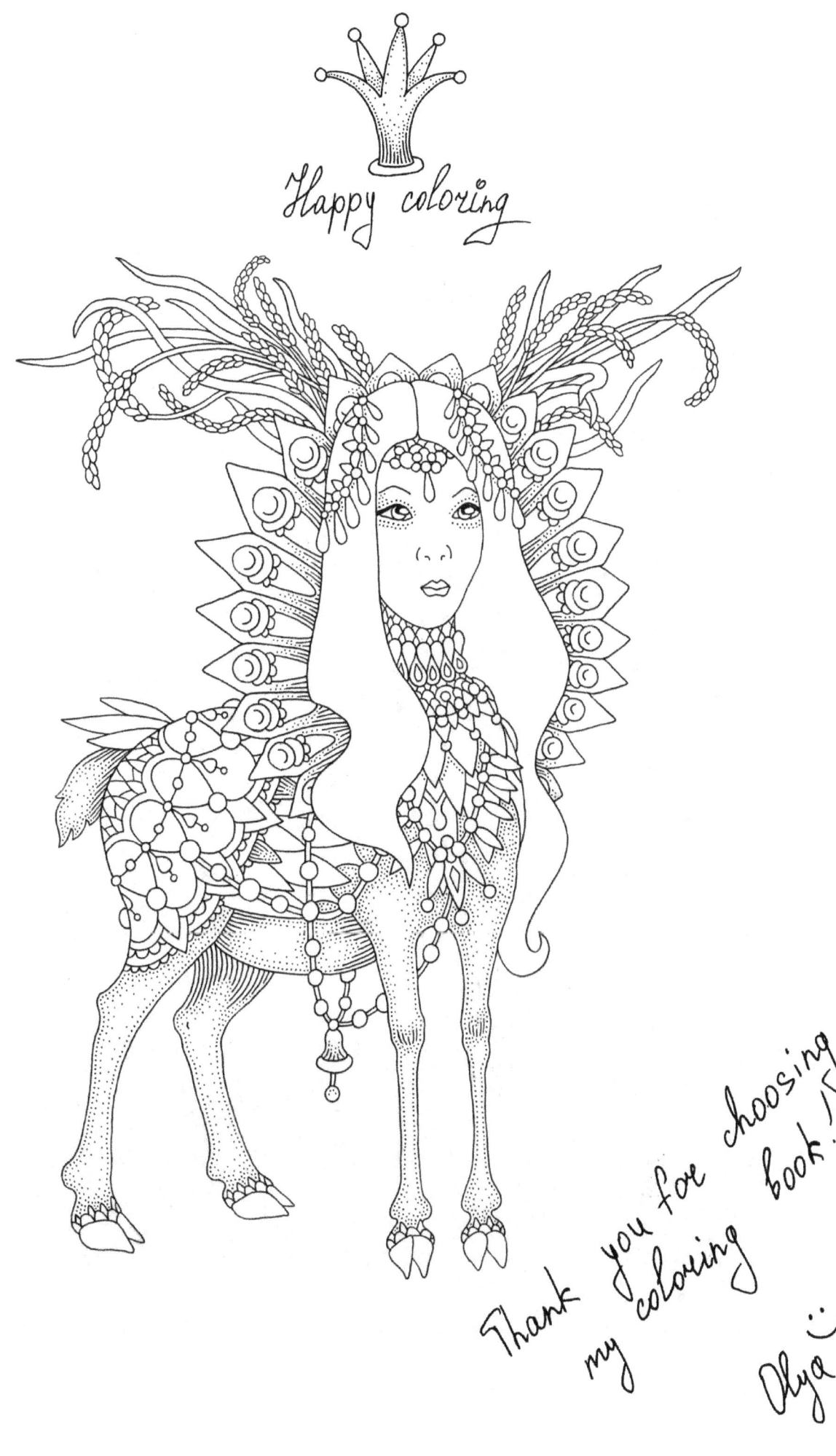

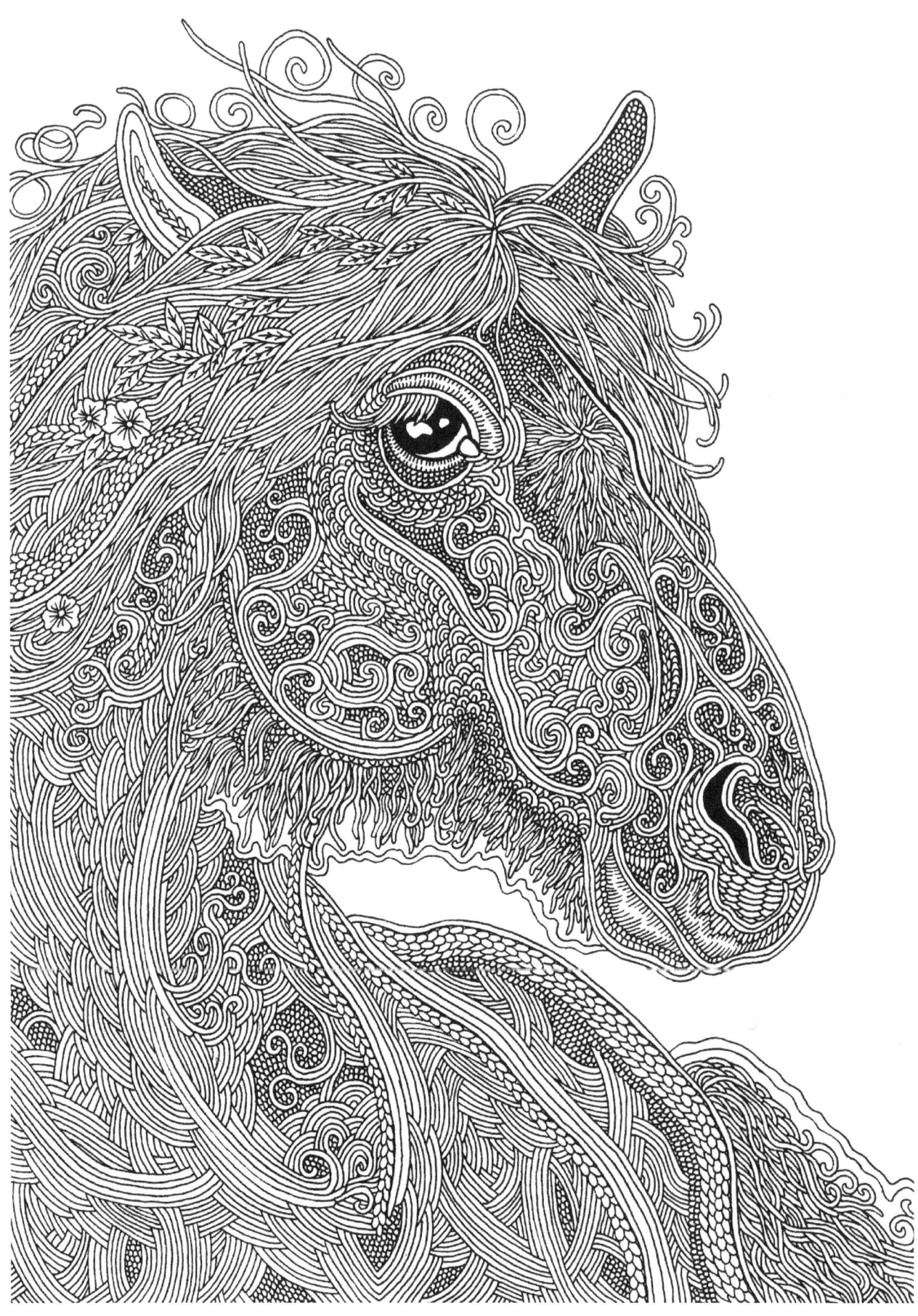

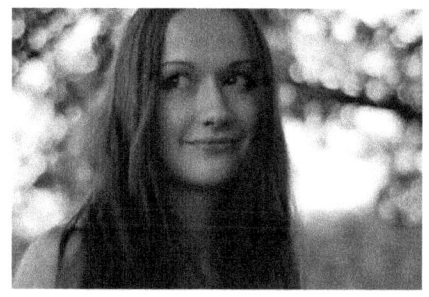

ABOUT THE AUTHOR

Olga Goloveshkina is a freelance artist and illustrator based in Moscow, Russia.
She graduated from the Institute of Business and Design.
Olga specializes in black ink doodles.
She is an author and illustrator coloring books for adults:
1. "The wind carries flowers"/"Veter unosit tsvety" (in Russian, 2015),
2. "Fox travel: Coloring book" (in English, 2016),
3. "Mounts" (in English, 2016),
4. "Mounts 2" (in English, 2016),
5. "Enchanted horses" (in English, 2016),
6. "Horse and Architecture" (in English, 2016),
7. "Alice in Wonderland Coloring Book" (in English, 2017),
8. "Mounts 3" zodiac coloring book (in English, 2017),
9. "Mounts 4" Halloween coloring book (in English, 2017),
10. "Mounts 5" Christmas coloring book (in English, 2017),
11. "The queens. Monsters. Werewolves. Goddesses." (in English, 2018).

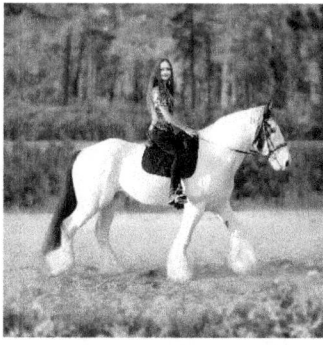

Author page on Amazon:
amazon.com/author/olgagoloveshkina
Site: http://olyagoloveshkina.jimdo.com
etsy.com/shop/OlyaColoringBook
Instagram:
@olyahitrayapanda

This book belongs to

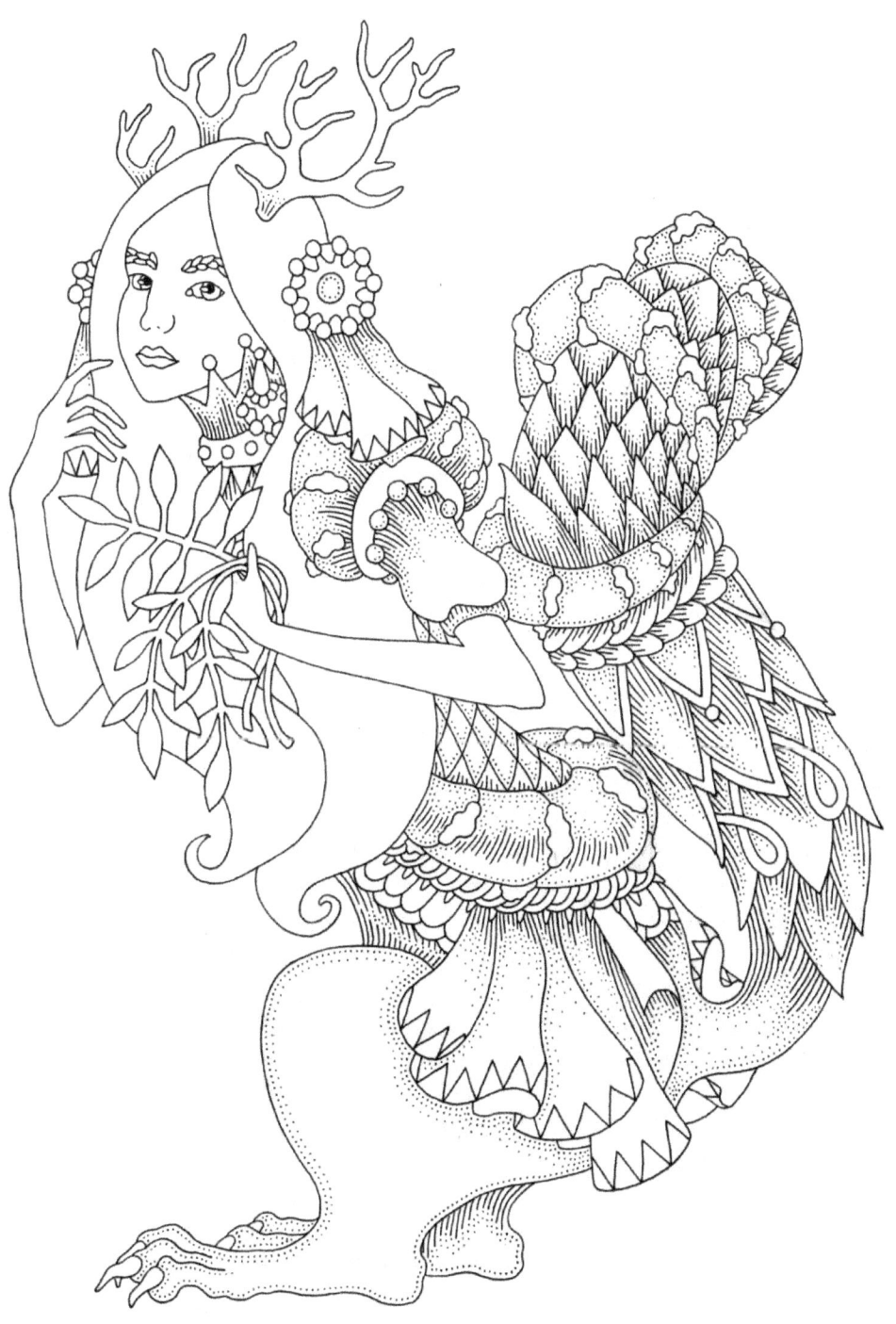

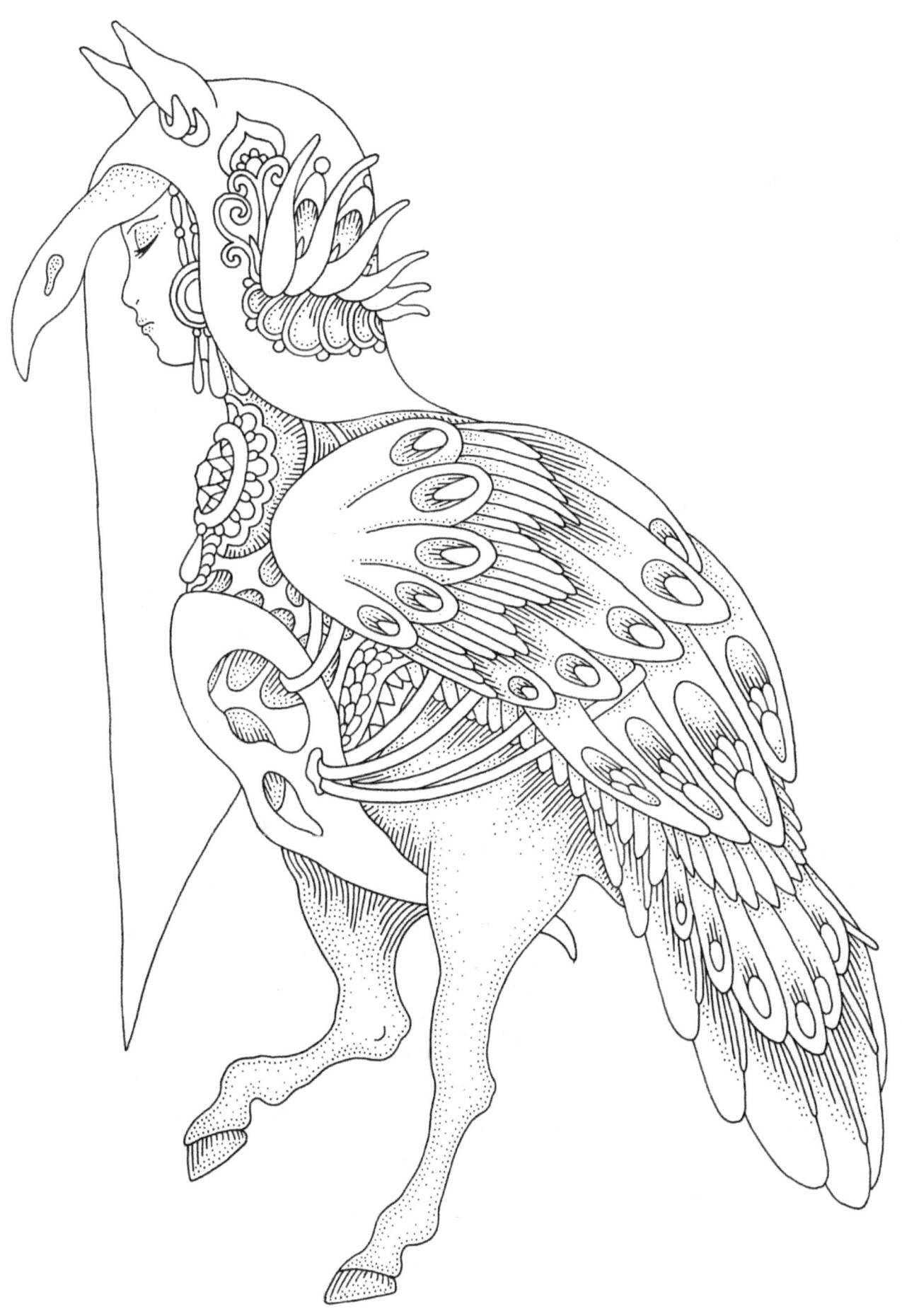

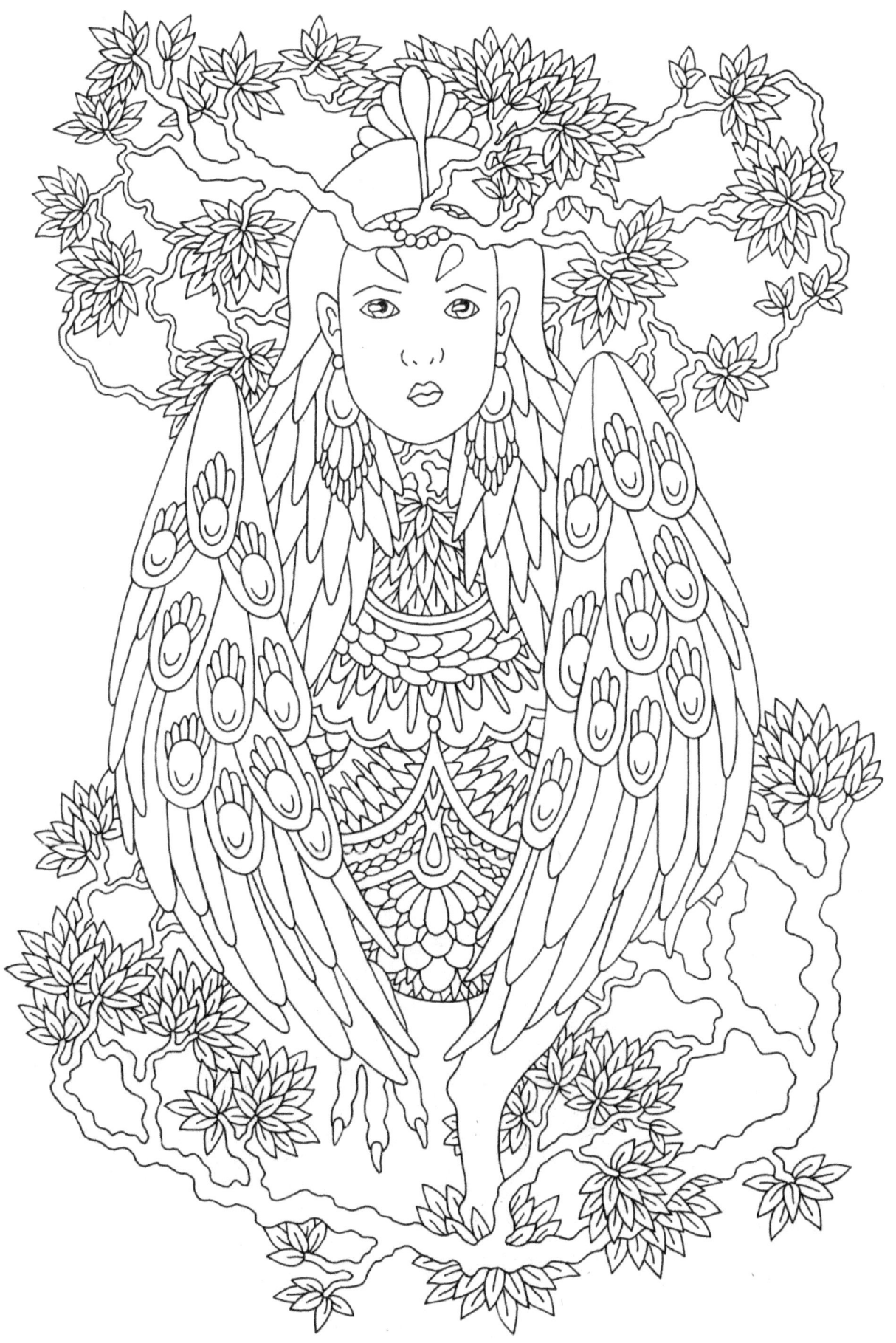

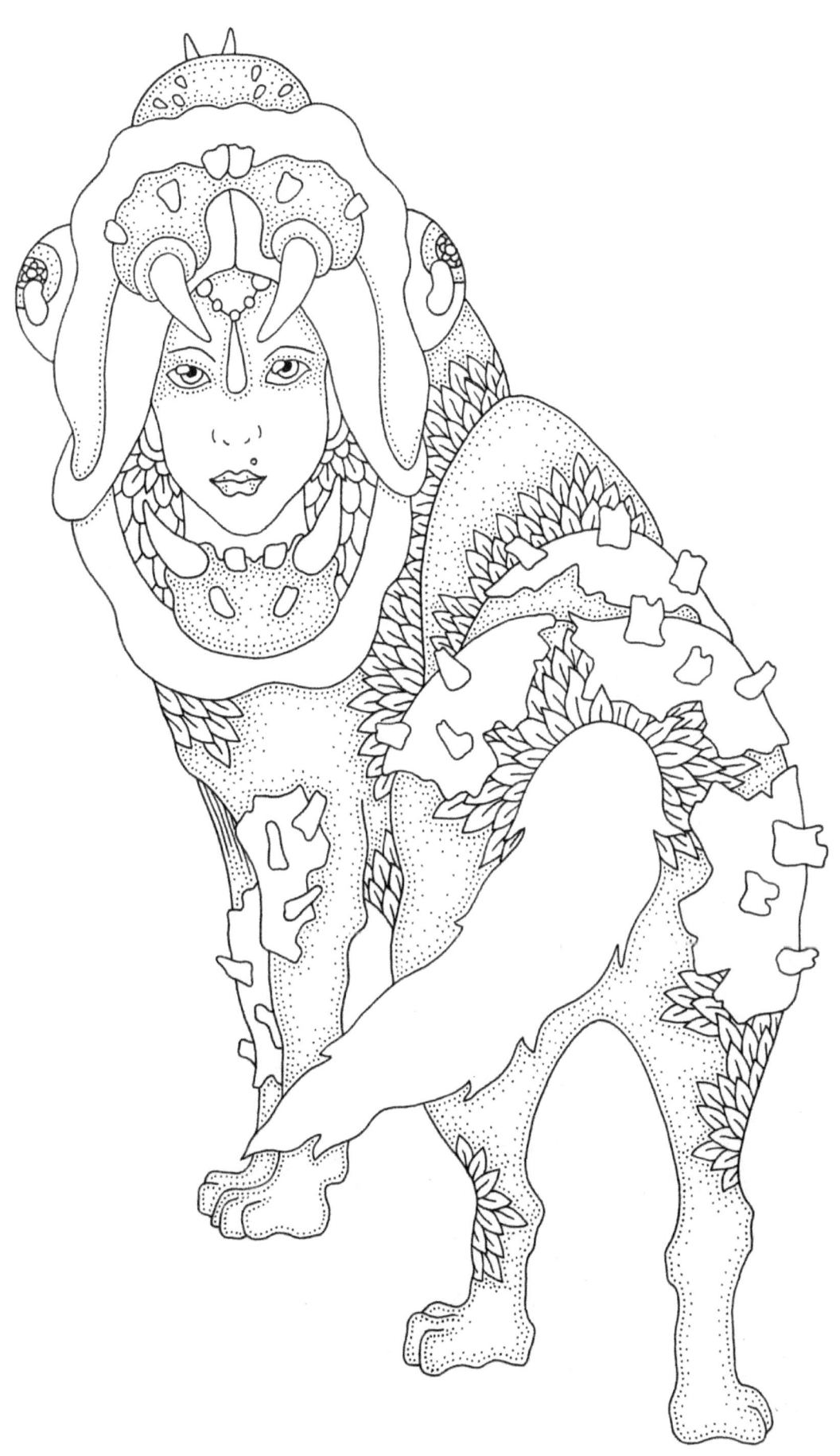

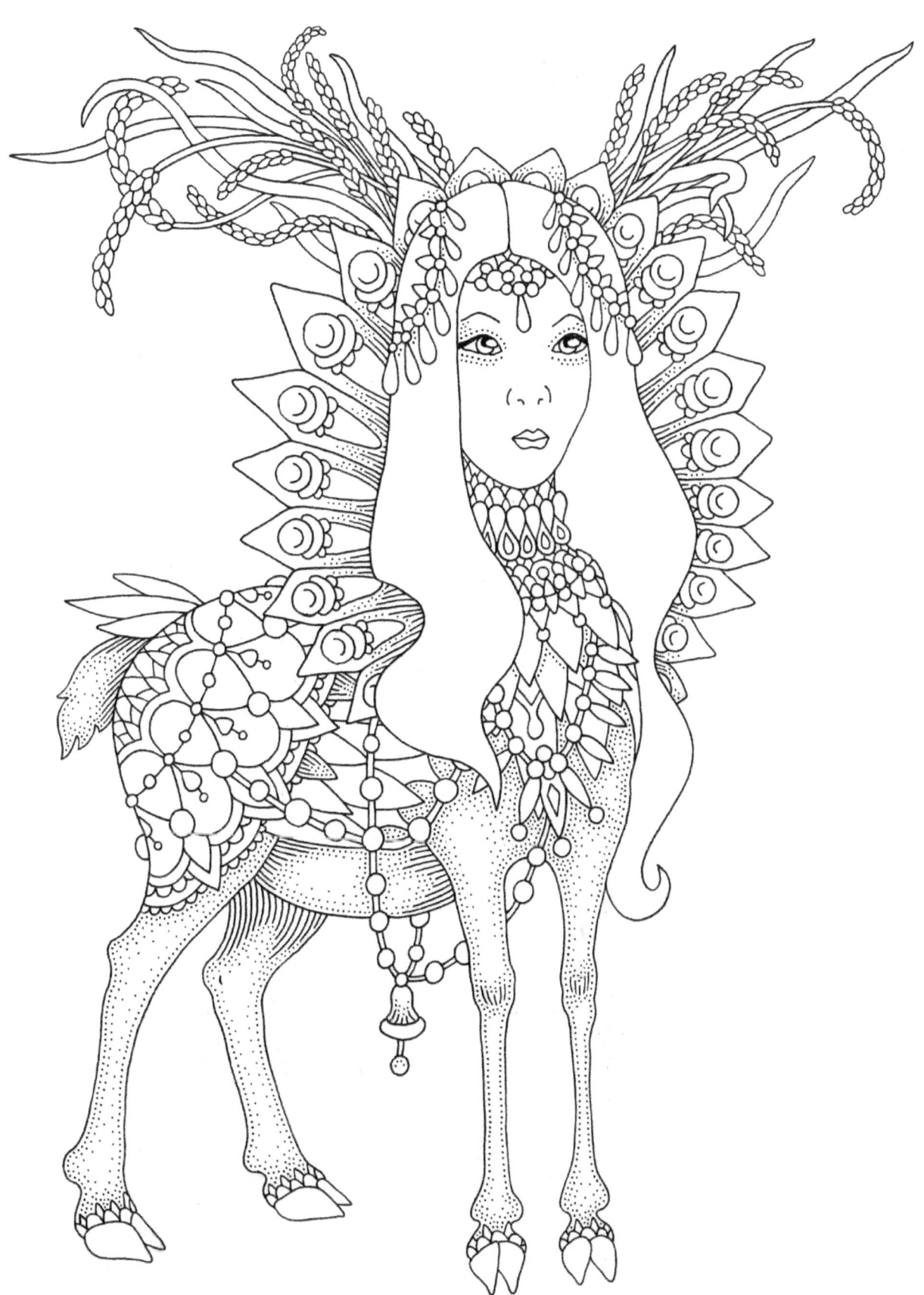

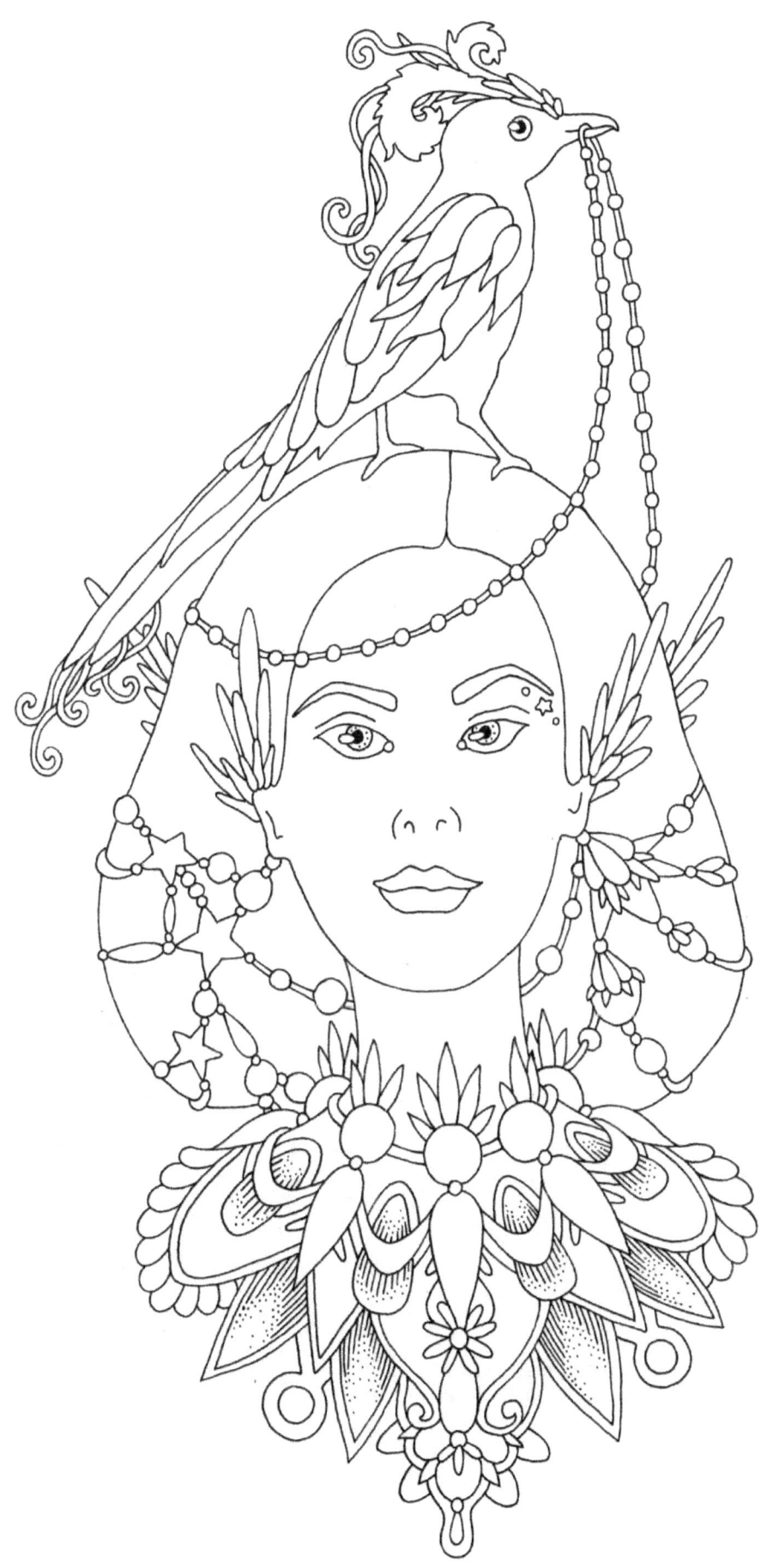

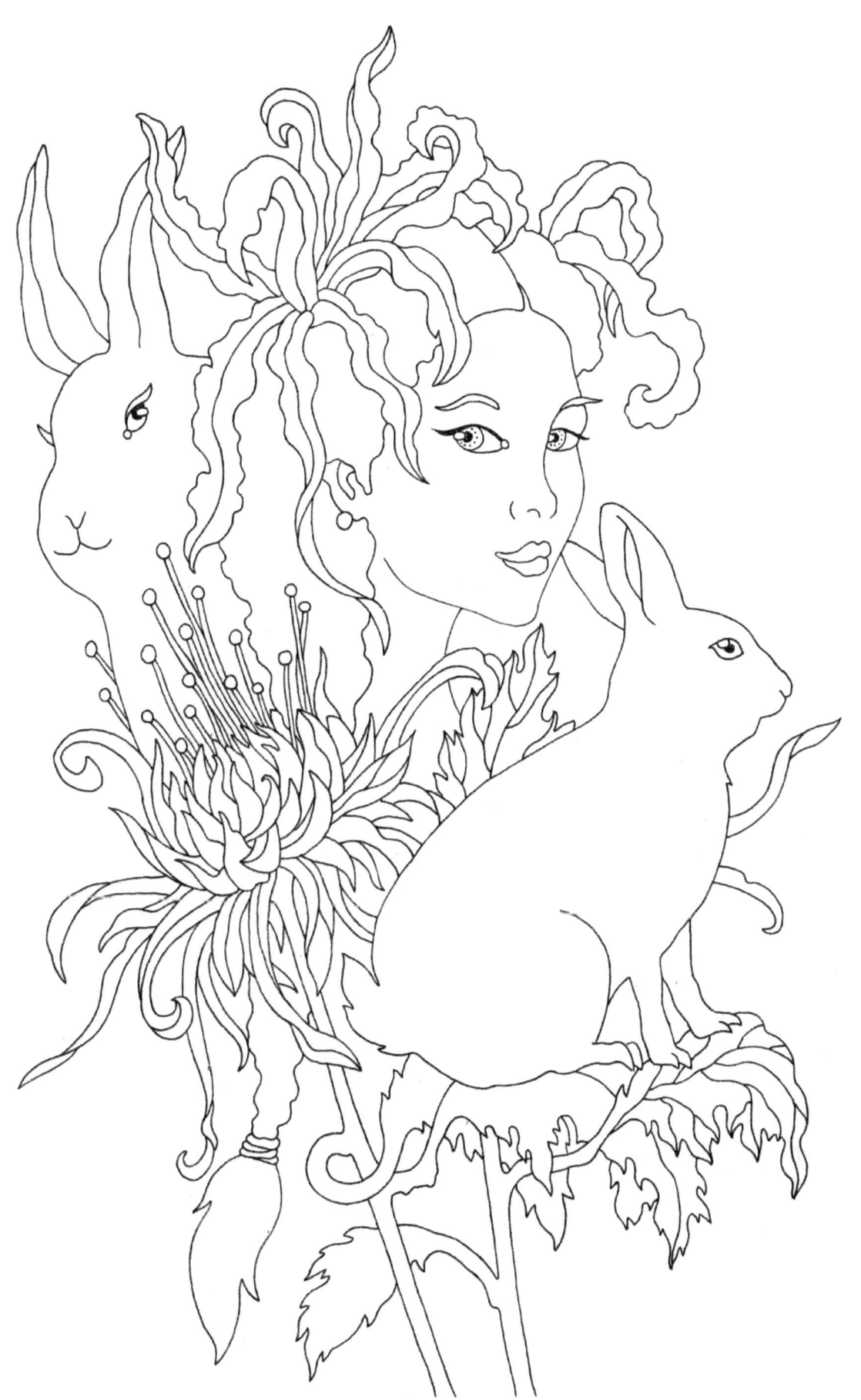

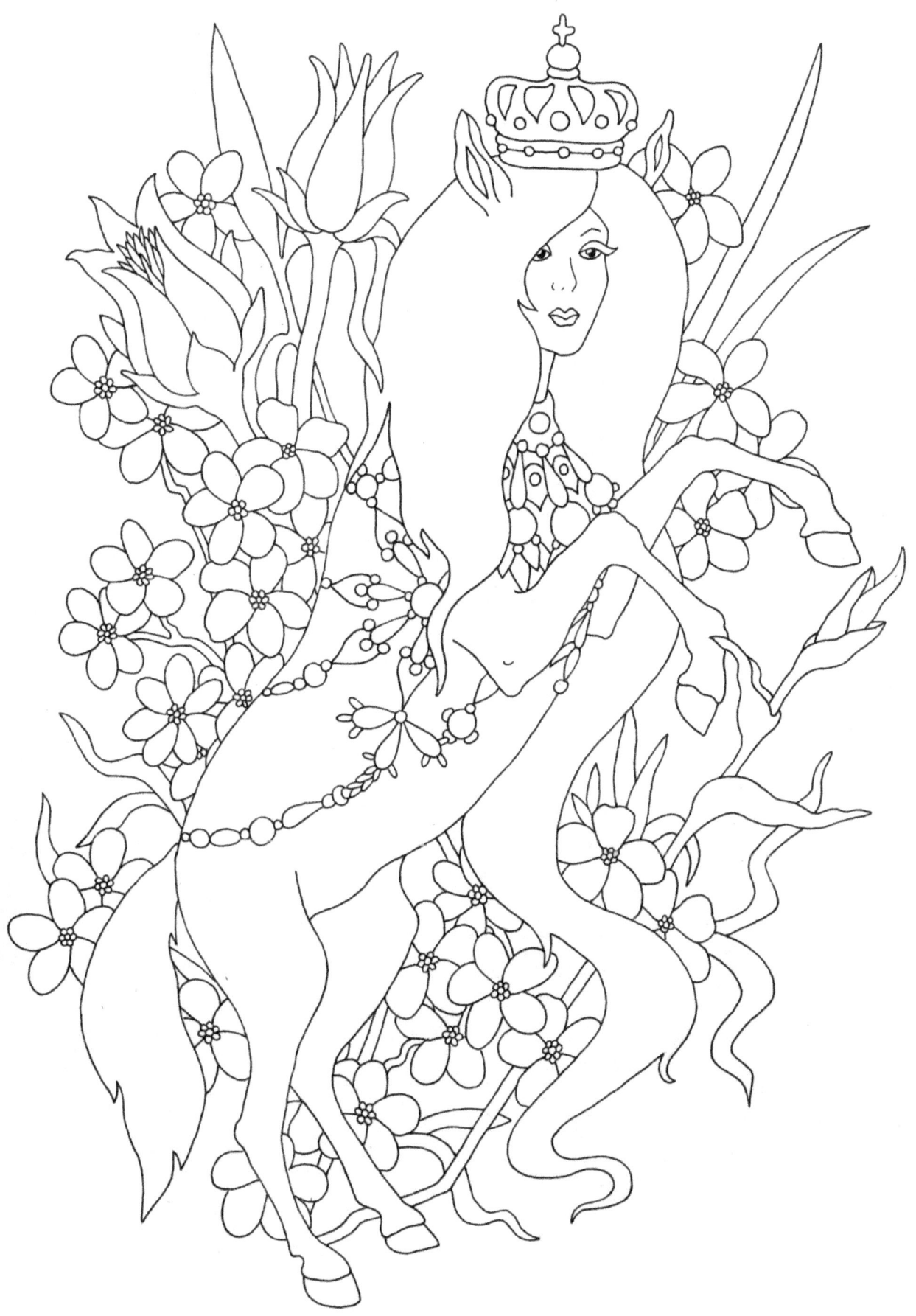

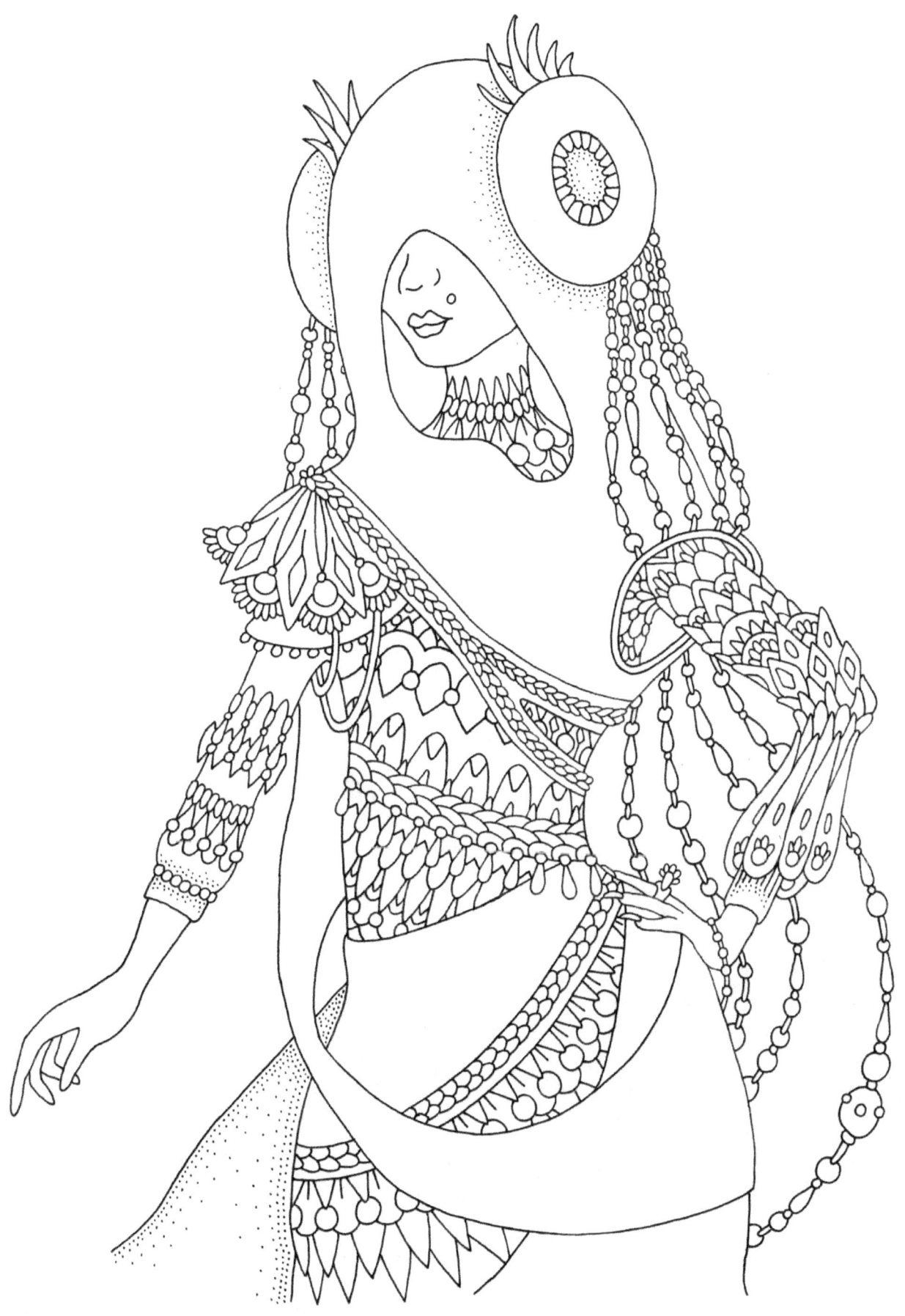

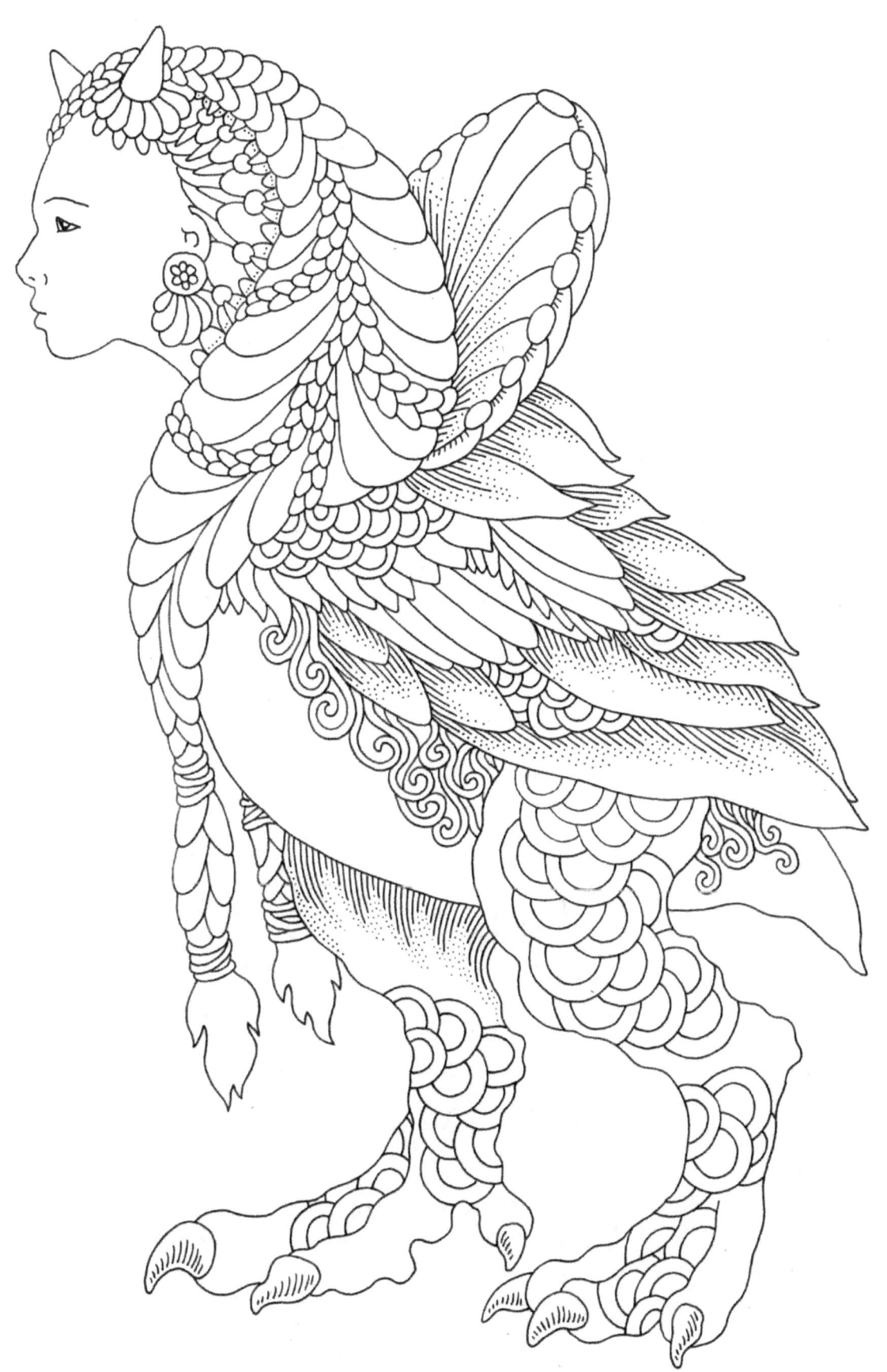

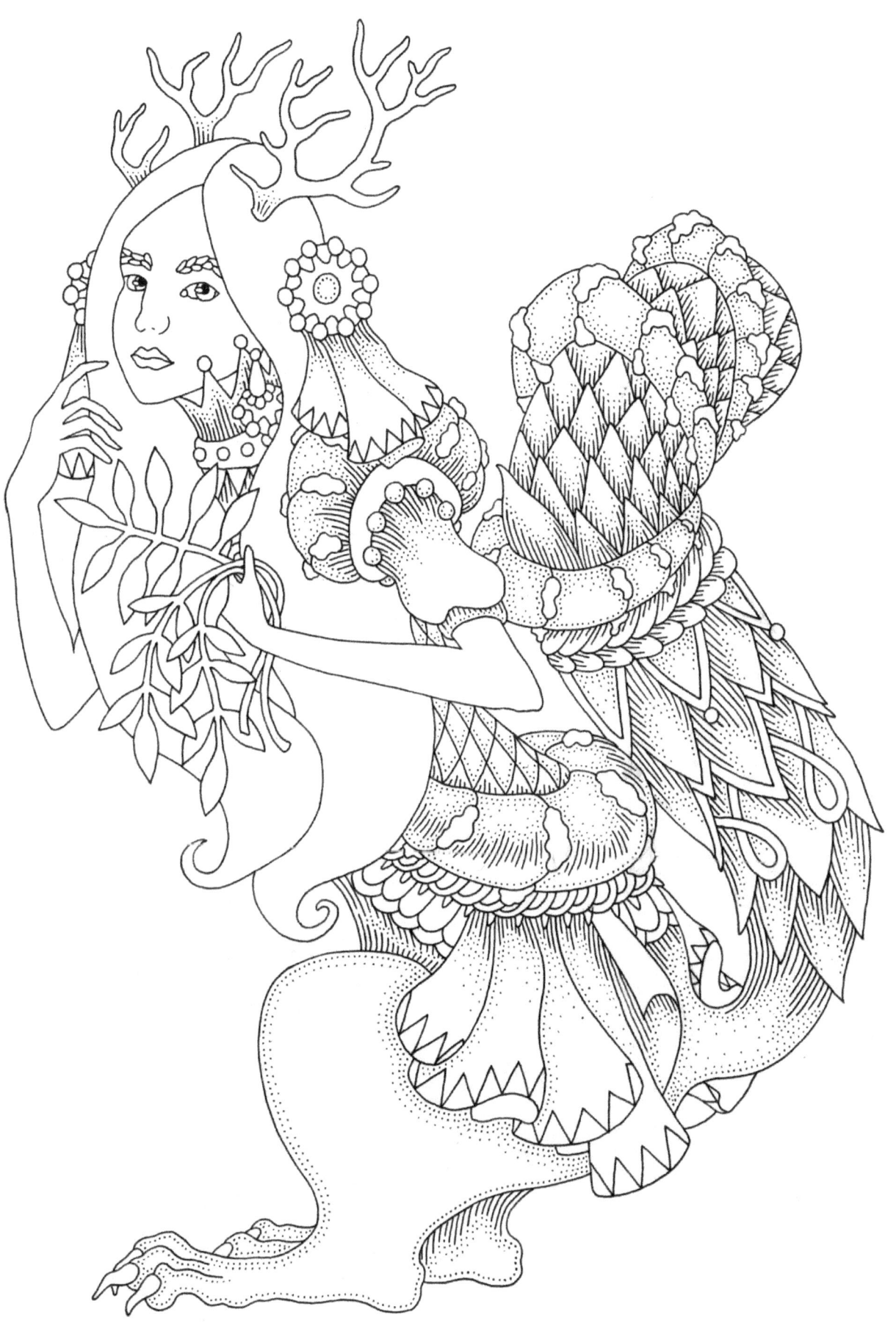

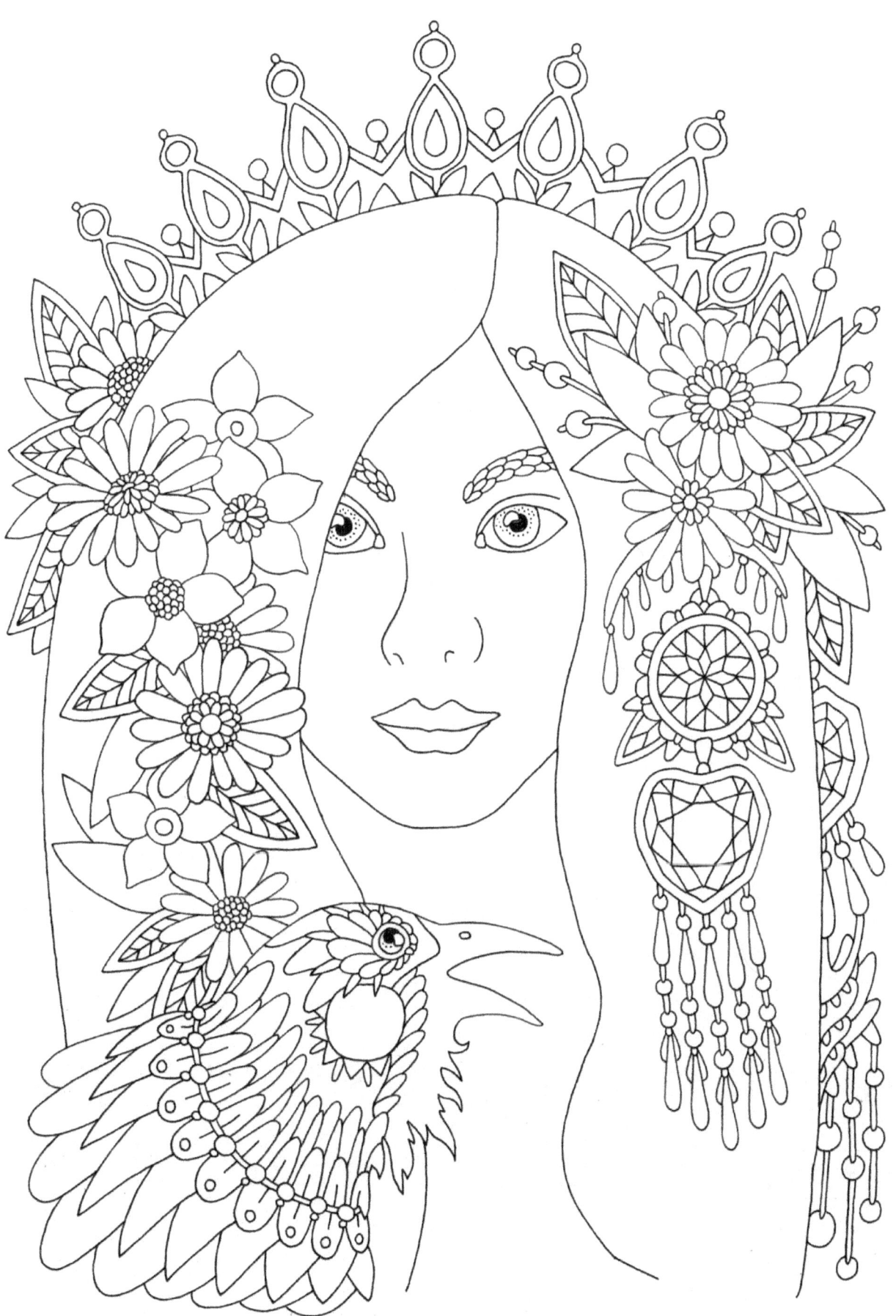

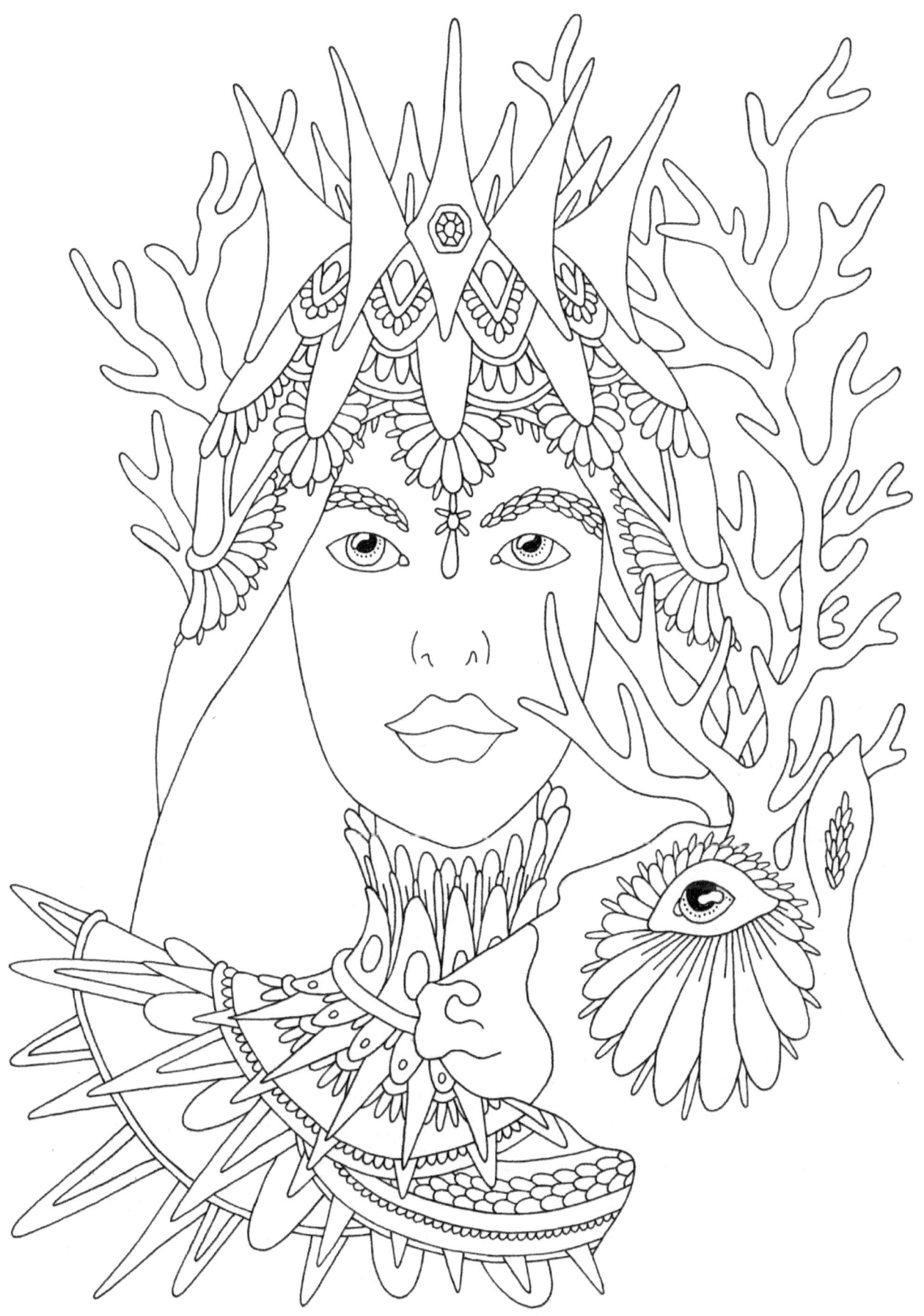

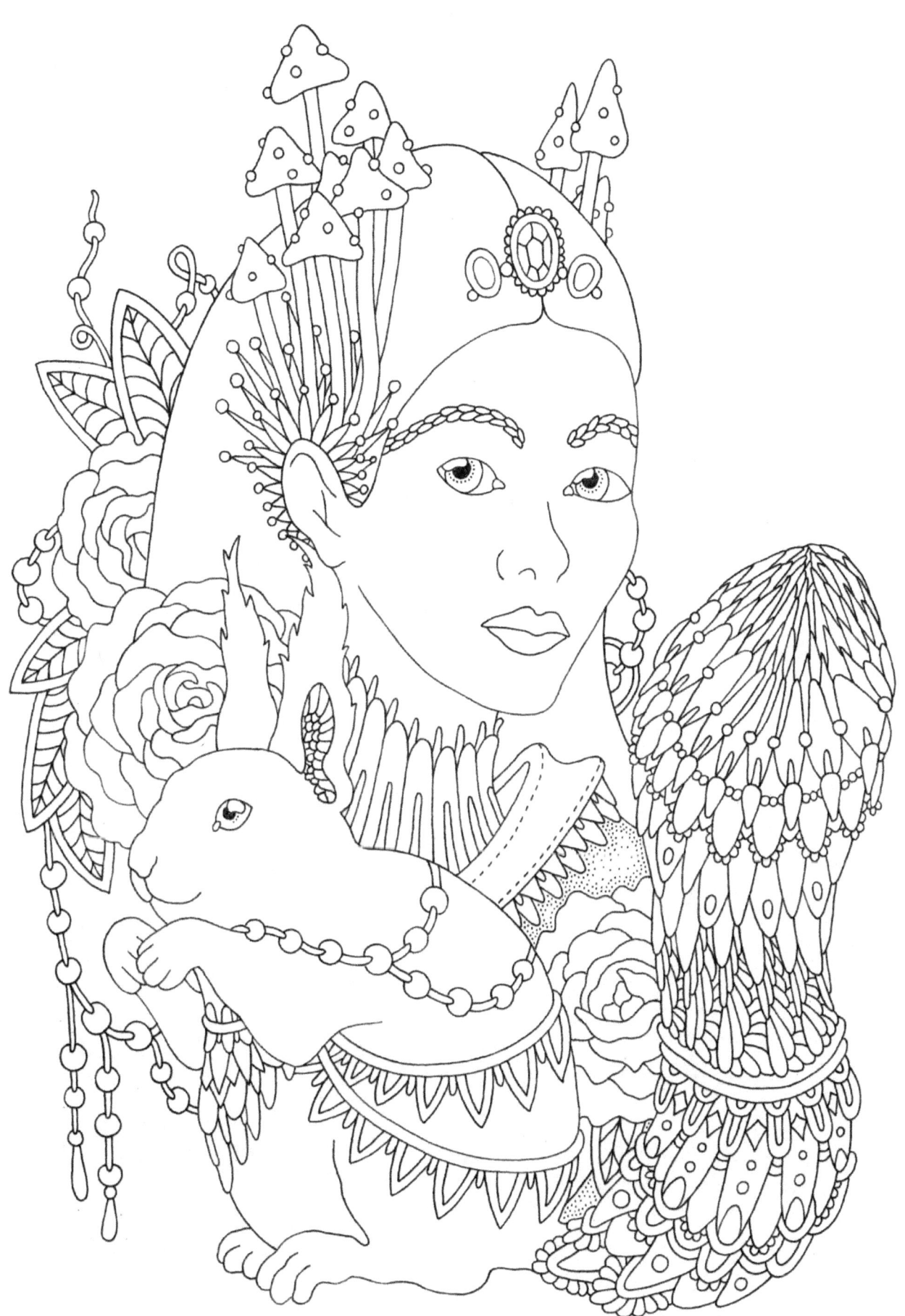

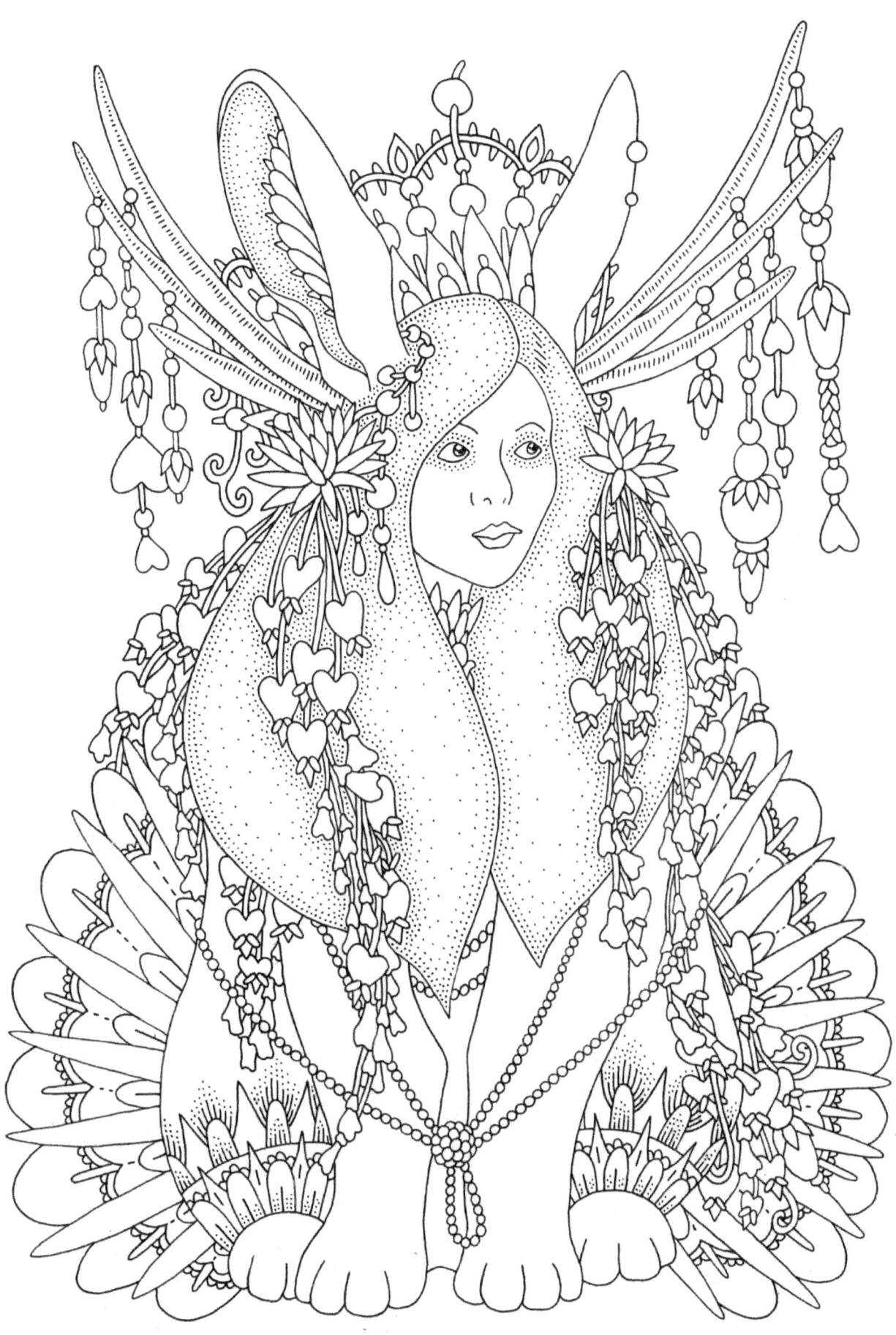

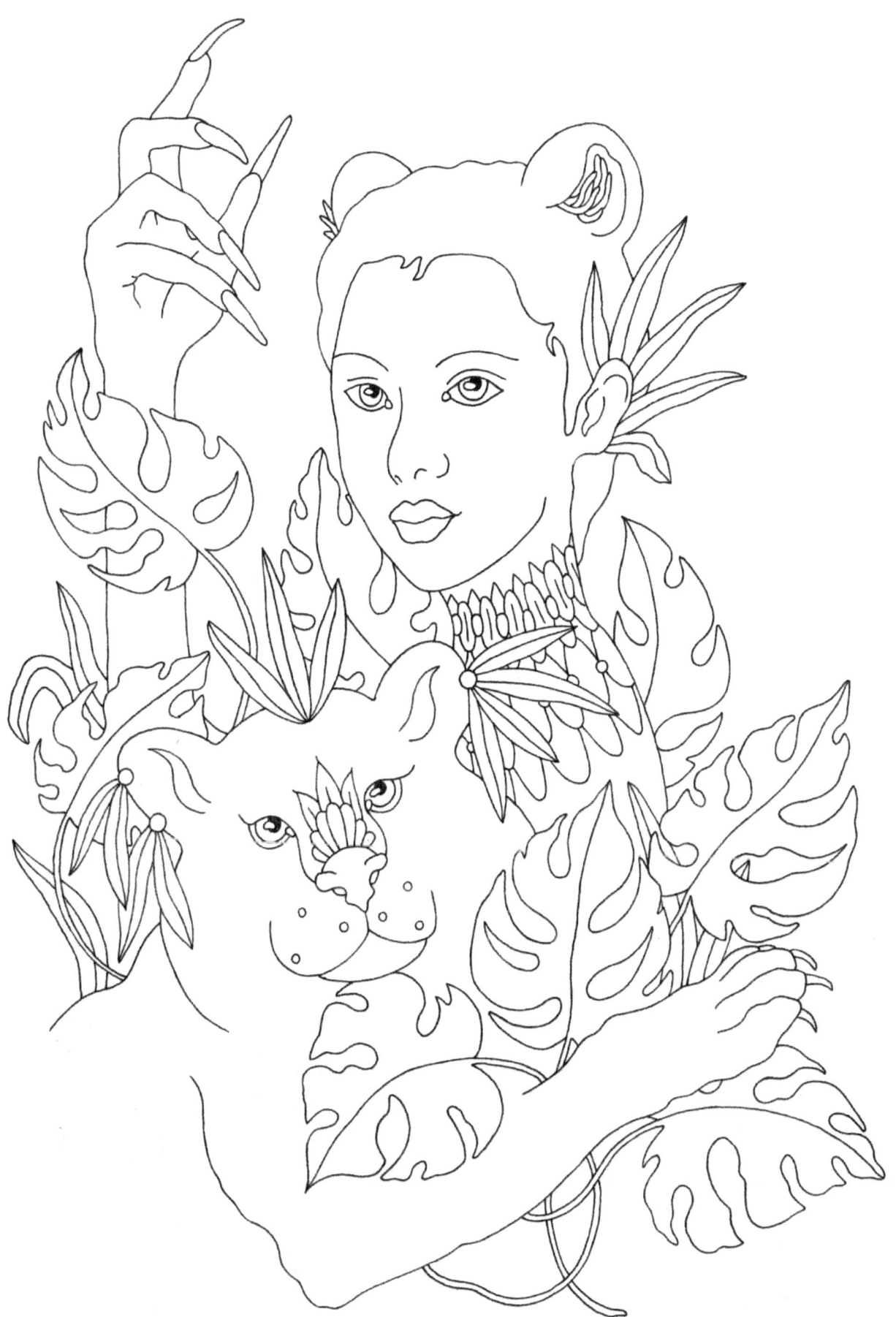

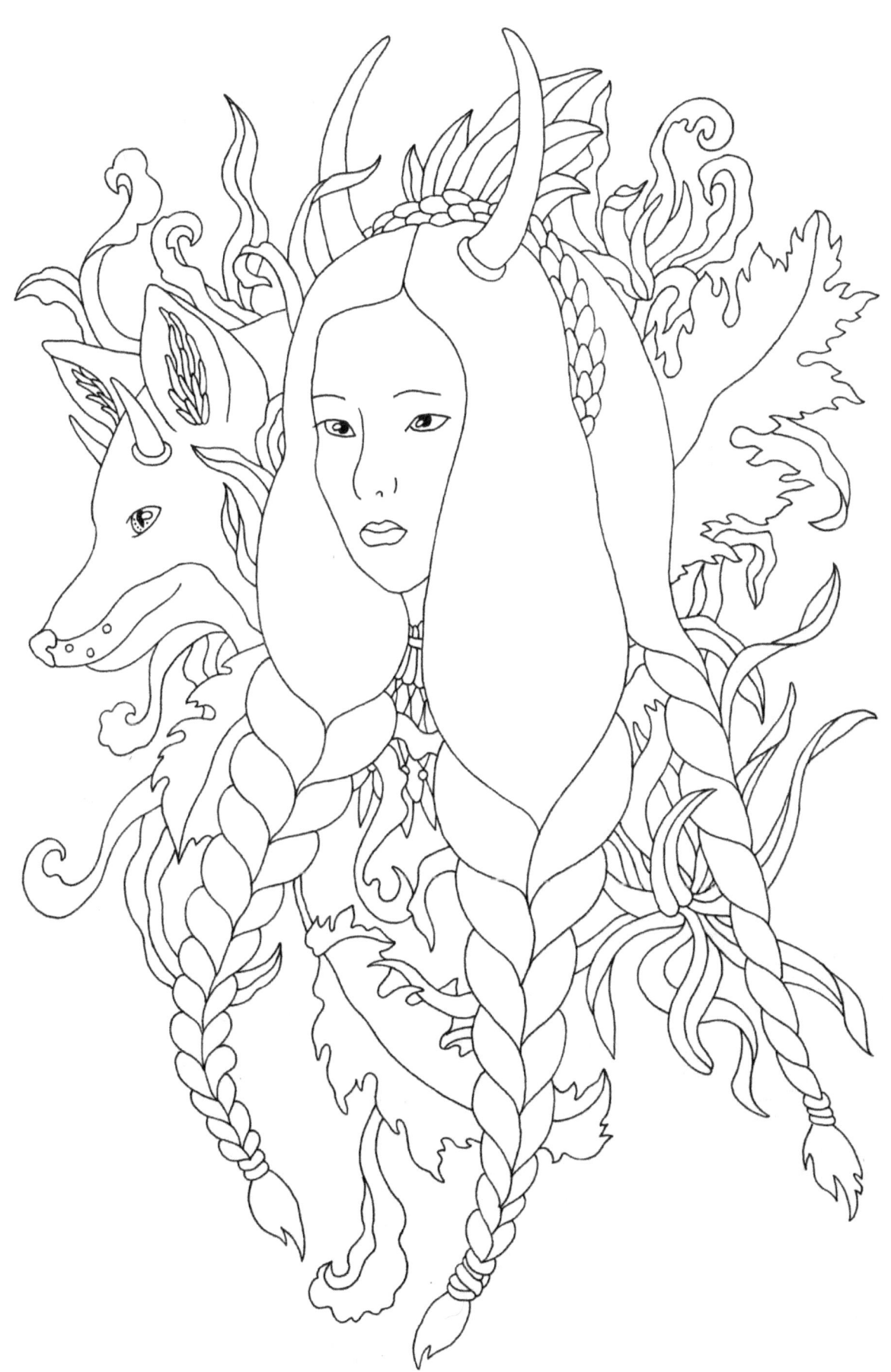

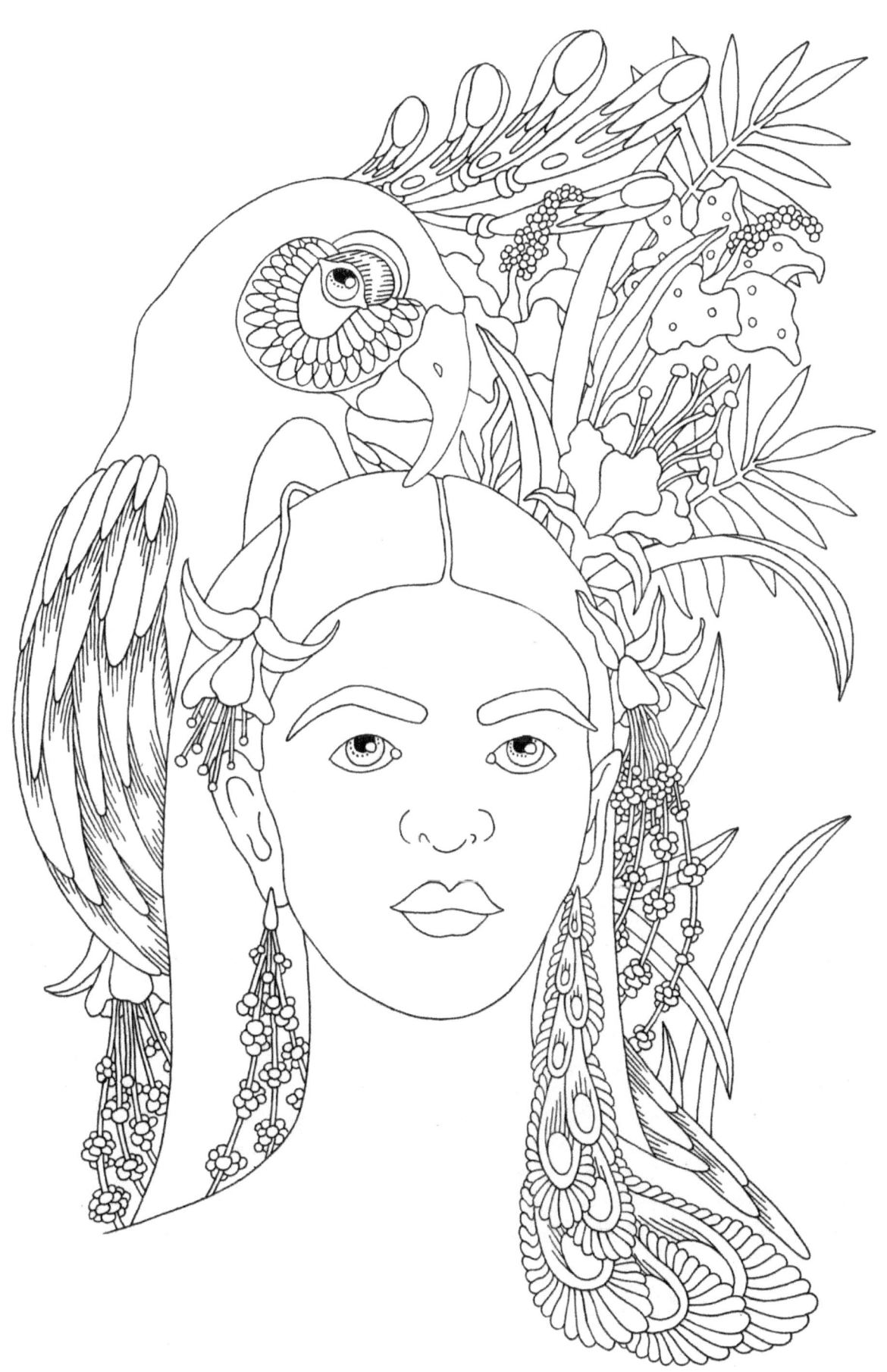

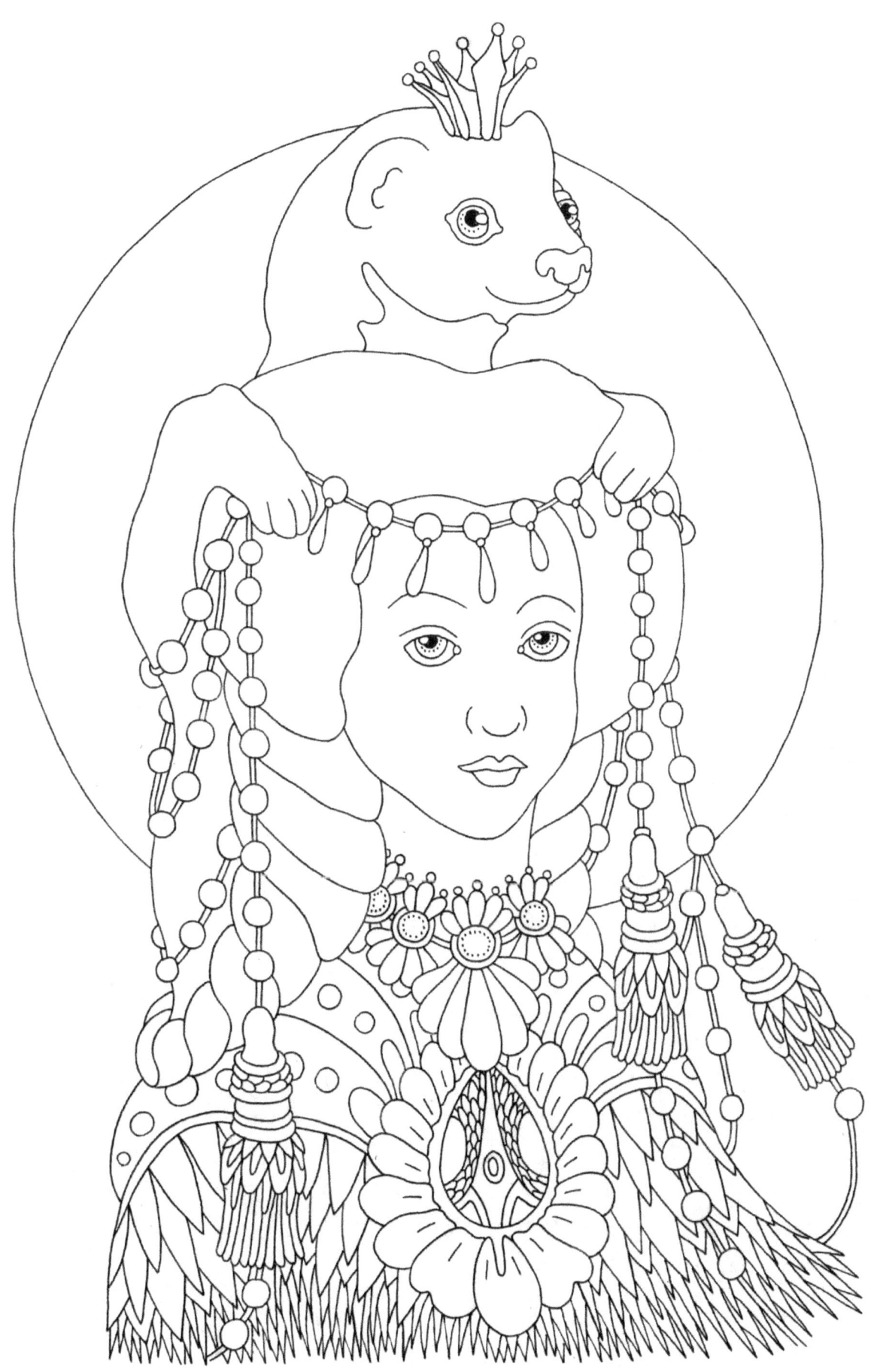

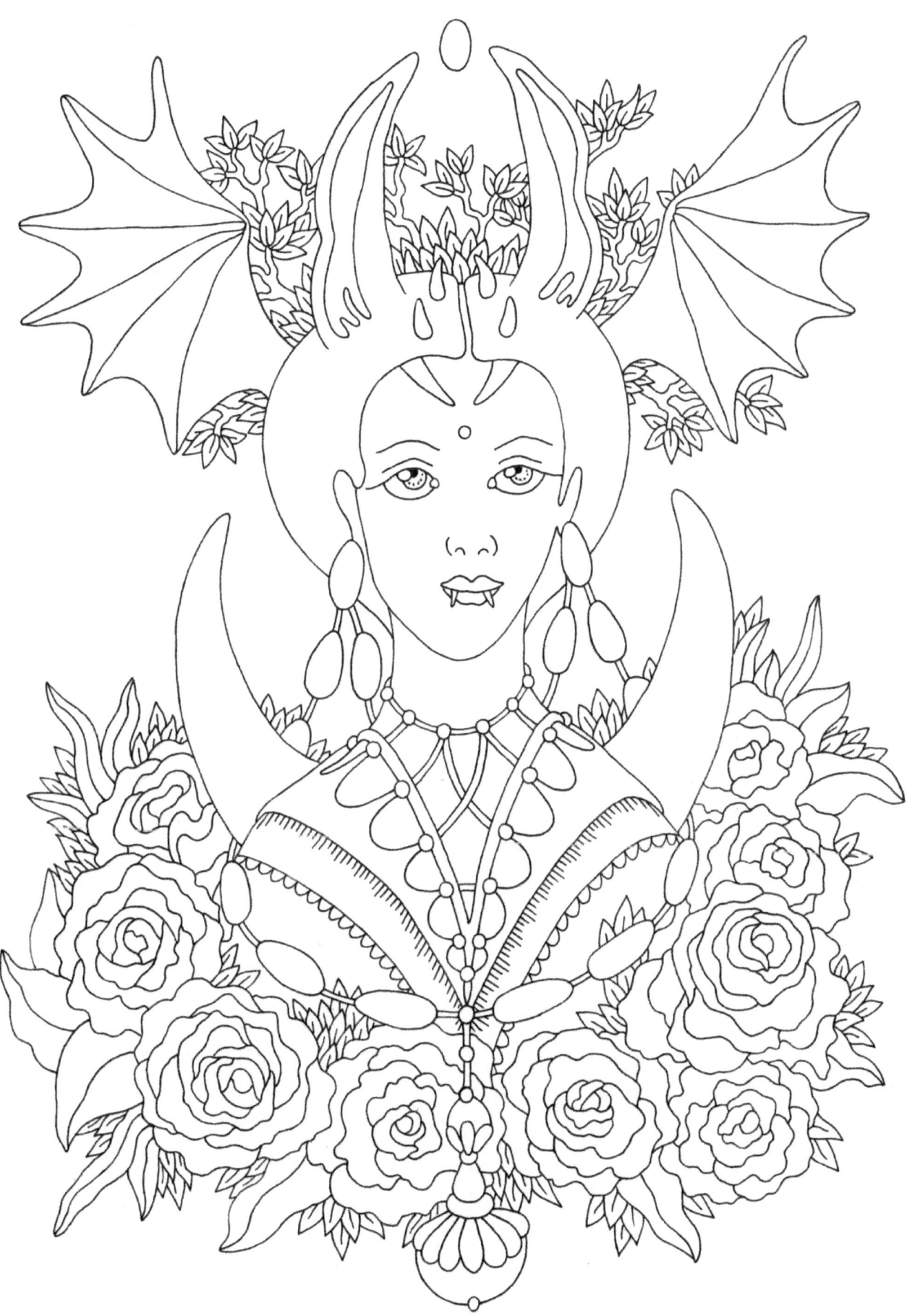

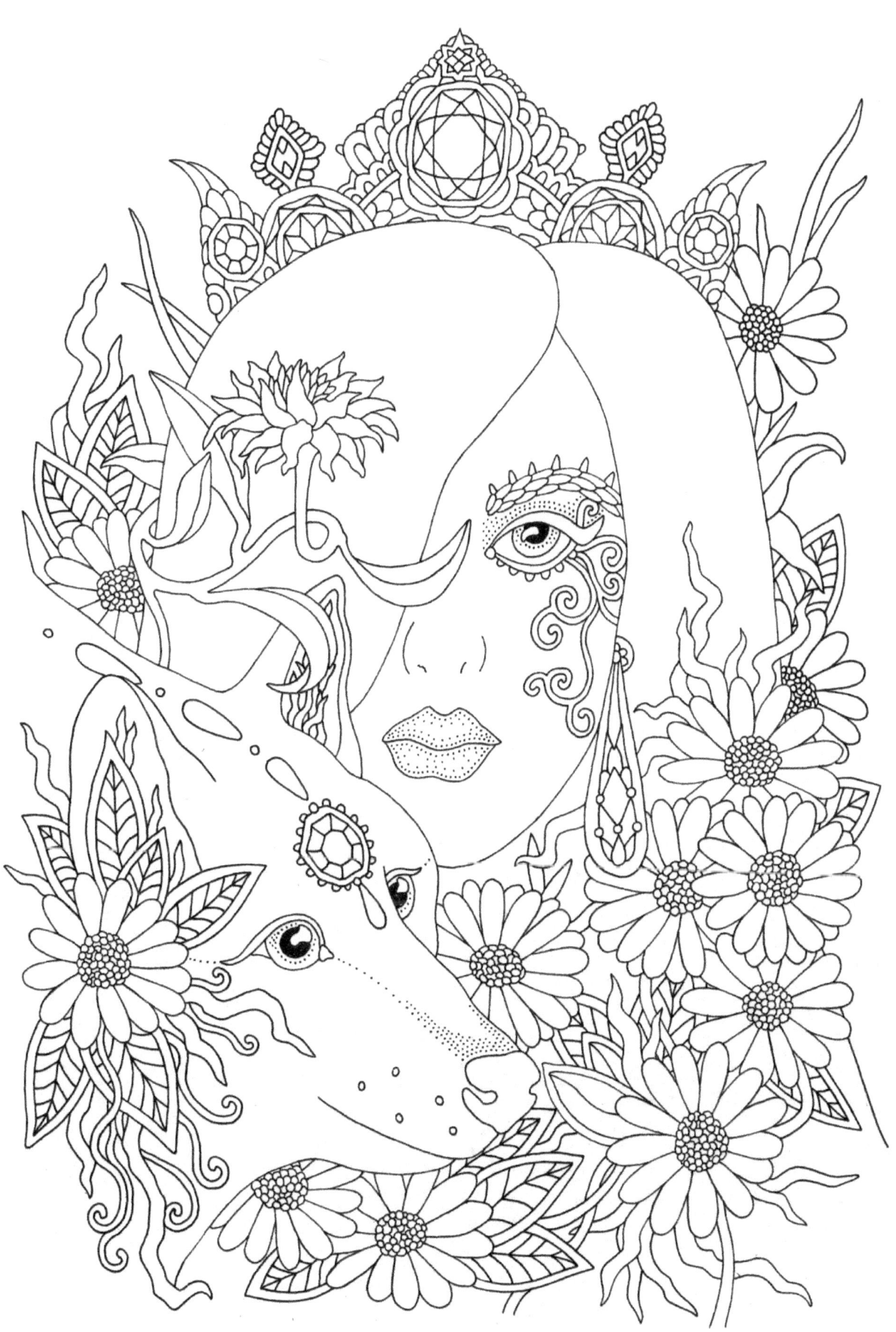

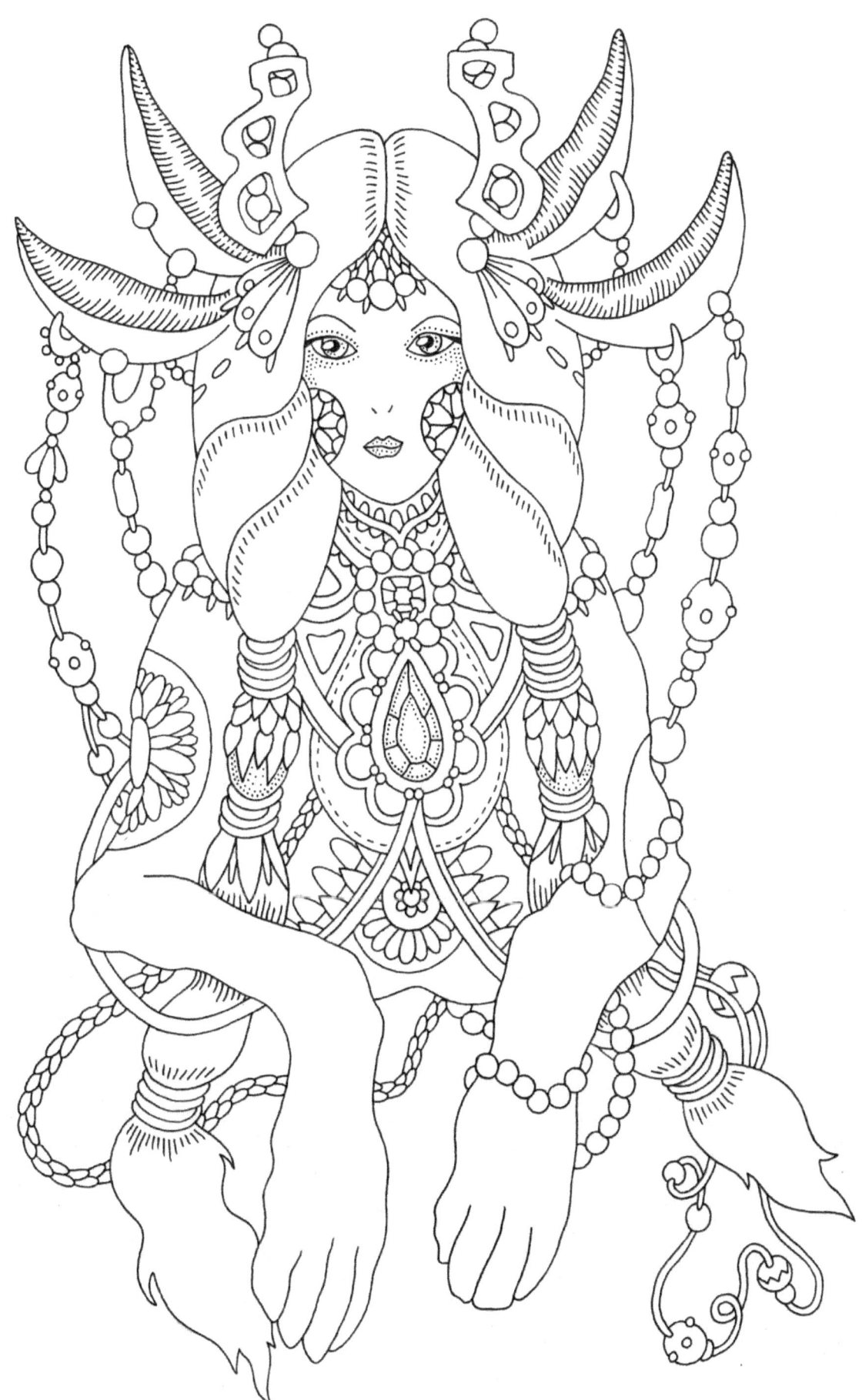

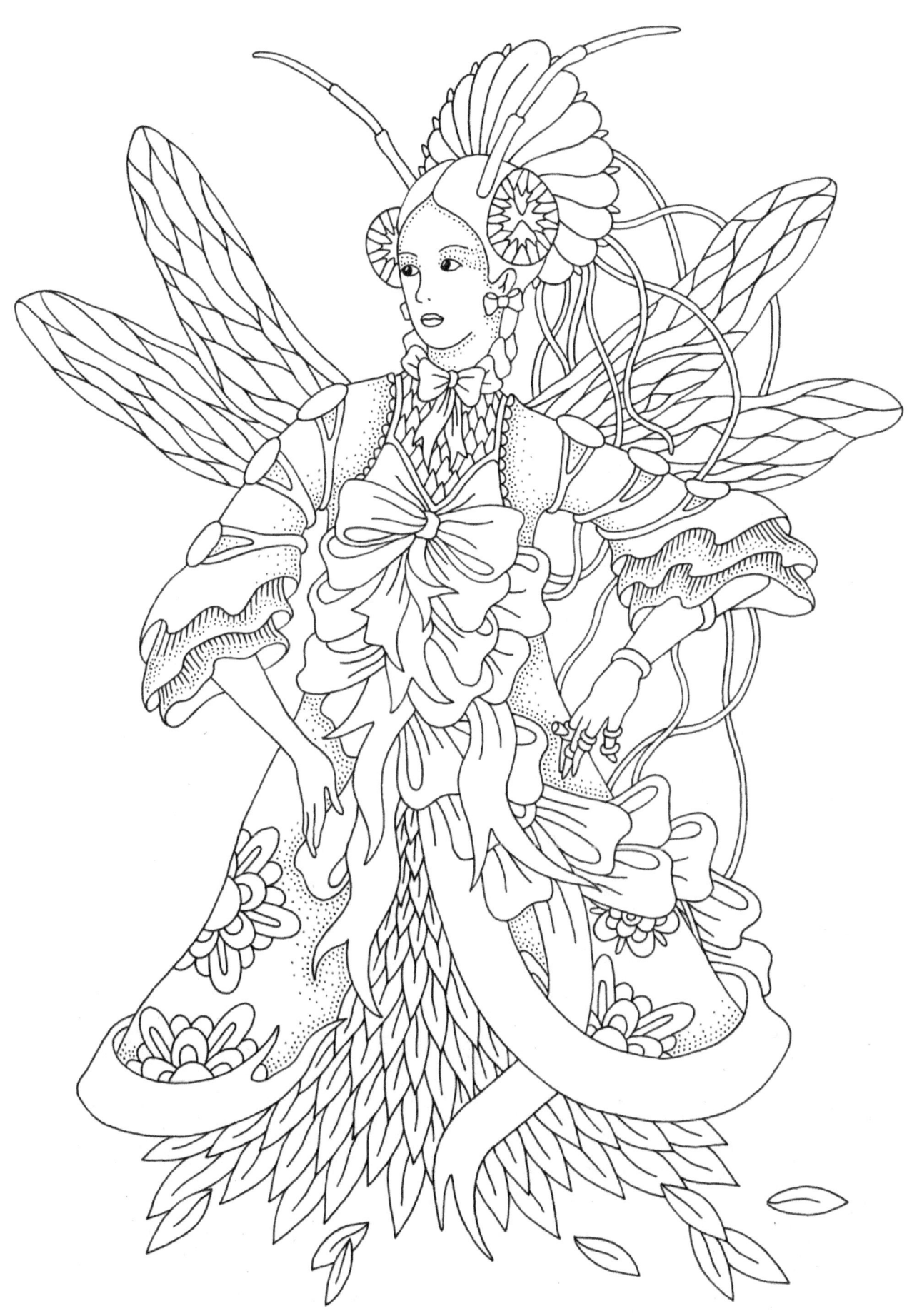

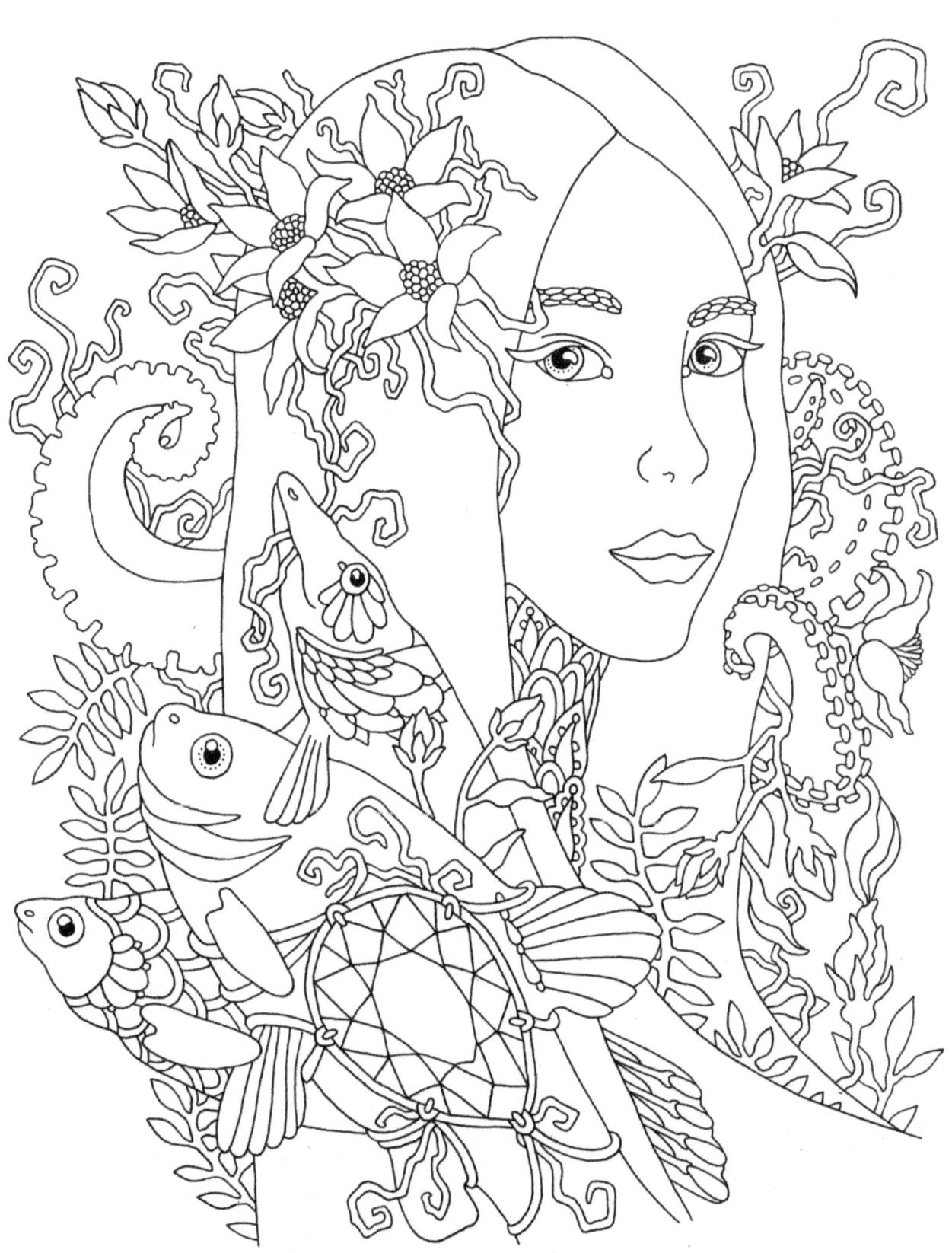

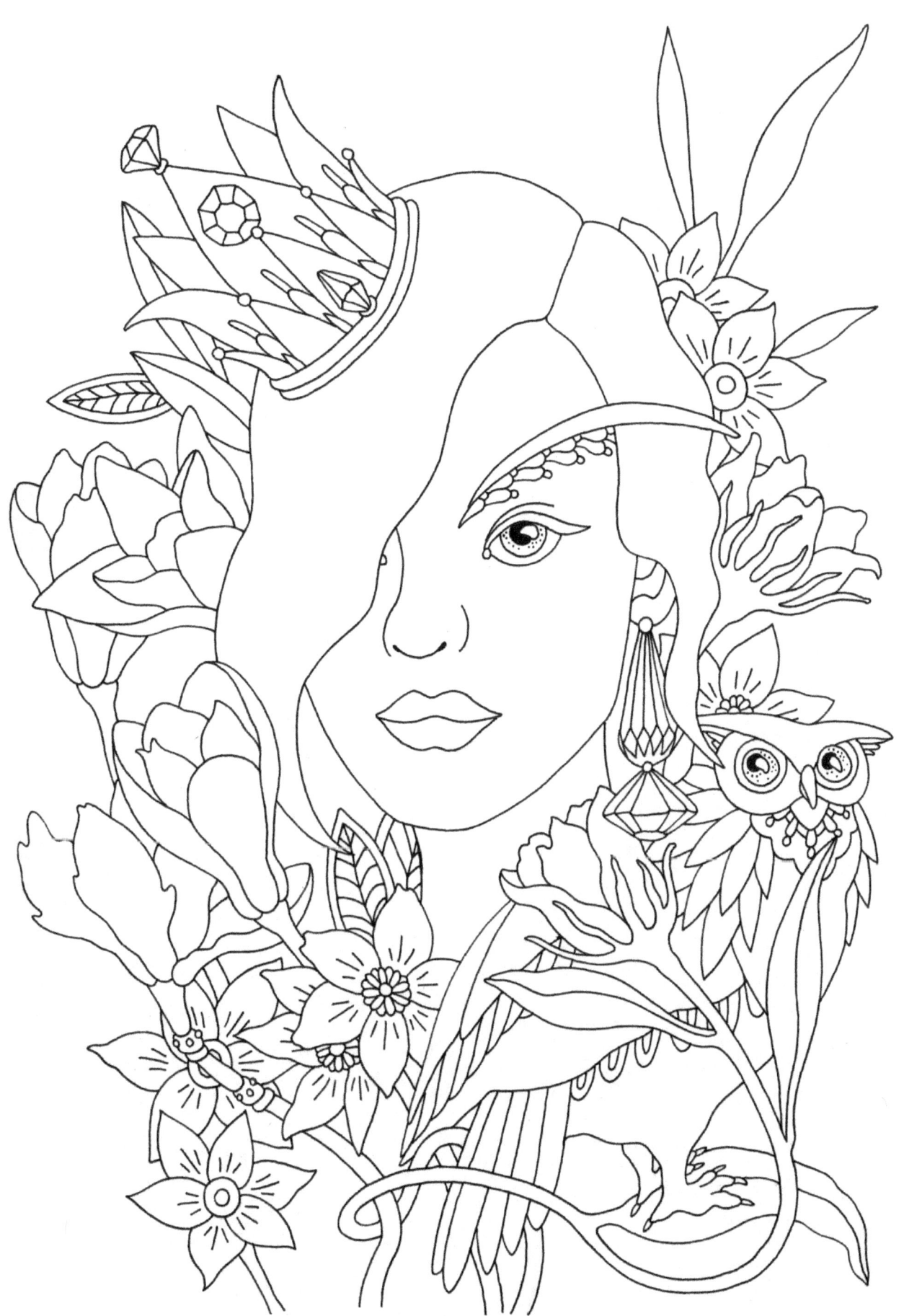

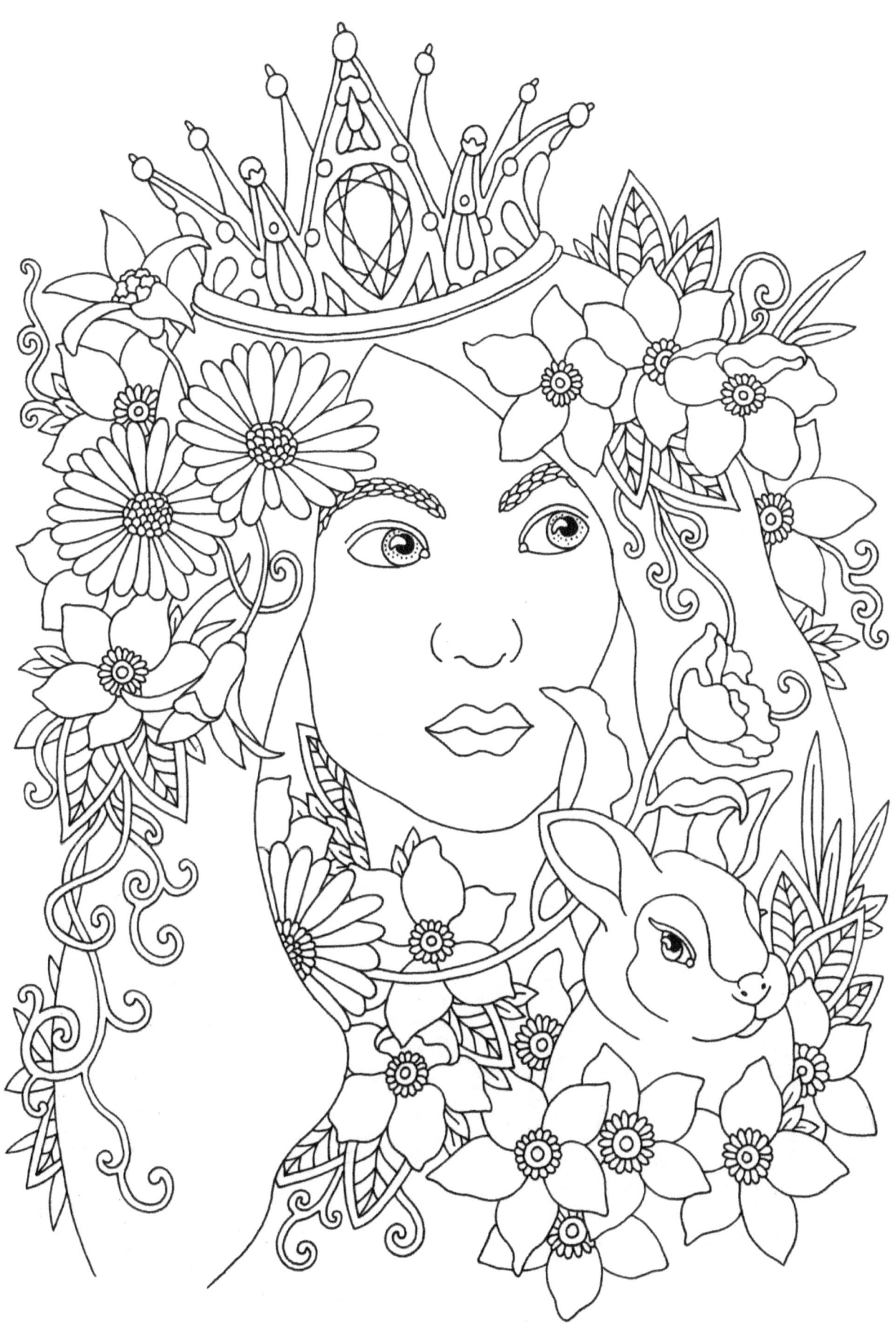

www.ingramcontent.com/pod-product-compliance
Lightning Source LLC
Chambersburg PA
CBHW062231220526

45471CB00009B/3436